...tern of Thi...

...d by Doro...

...nceptio...

A new pattern in evange... inter-church cooperation is reported ... detail by C. T. Itty. Mr. Itty, a Syrian Orthodox church member in India, was called to service in the Indonesian Church of Presbyterian communion. A new idea in the "pattern of things to come" is cooperation with non-Christians of goodwill. A pattern for Southeast Asia, proposed by Dr. David Moses, is one of the high points in this book, as it was at the conference. It is a pattern that sweeps aside denominational differences, crosses national boundaries, and recognizes that the task of the church can never be fulfilled except in united witness. It is a pattern that carries out the gospel injunction: "That they may all be one; even as thou, Father, art in me..."

After each chapter is a set of "thought-provokers"—questions that will open avenues for discussion and interpretation.

Dorothy McConnell, editor of these "essays," has written a preface, personal-interest stories introducing each chapter, and a summary at the end of the book. She says, "This book is a tale of compulsion, the compulsion to share the knowledge of Jesus Christ. . . . The pattern of things to come is founded on the belief in the power of all men and women . . . to understand truth. Whence cometh the power? The answer that the Christian gives to that question makes the peoples of the world one in spiritual heritage."

PATTERN OF THINGS TO COME

compiled by
Dorothy McConnell
in cooperation with the
Executive Staff
of the
Division of Foreign Missions
National Council of the Churches
of Christ in the U. S. A.
published for
the Division of Foreign Missions
by Friendship Press
New York
1955

pattern of things to come

COPYRIGHT, 1955, BY FRIENDSHIP PRESS, INC.
PRINTED IN THE UNITED STATES OF AMERICA
Library of Congress Catalog Card Number: 55-10430

"In the midst of the epoch-making changes in the world,
the world mission of the Church must change. But how and when?
We need wisdom. Even more we need faith and courage
and the spirit of adventure of the early Church as we seek
to find the pattern of things to come."

Raymond A. Dudley

CONTENTS

THE APPROACH

It is well for the reader to keep in mind how the word "pattern" is used in the following pages. It is not used in the sense of a natural pattern caused by circumstances over which man has no control, such as the pattern of leaves on the grass cast by sun shining through the branches of a tree. It is used, rather, in the sense of a pattern that can be cut out by man to fit the needs of a growing world. As in any figure of speech used by several men, the meaning is obscured now and again in these pages. The editor, however, has kept to the second meaning in selecting the comments and questions that have been gathered around the main sections of the book.

This is done in the hope that each comment, each question may suggest how the pattern should be cut, and that the reader, by the time he is ready to lay the book down, will have a fairly clear perception of what pattern will fit —along with necessary modifications here and there—the things to come.

PREFACE

During the month of November, 1954, the Division of Foreign Missions of the National Council of the Churches of Christ met in Boston to look at the pattern of things to come in missions. The discussions centered around papers that had been prepared, panels, and remarks from the floor. The participation, from the floor and from the platform, was by national Christians as well as Christians of the United States. All participants were aware of the revolutionary atmosphere in which the missionary movement lives today. Most of them recognized that, whether the revolution expresses itself in orderly or violent change in the countries they serve, the revolution itself is an outgrowth of man's desire to achieve a good life for himself. They also recognized that that desire is channeled into action, good or bad, toward getting that life.

Here a very interesting development was brought out. In some cases men working for the good life have forgotten themselves in the cause of a good life for all. They have, non-Christians as they may have been, given such dedication to the work that their behavior partakes of some aspects of religion itself.

In the old days it was the mission movement, usually, that was developing the land, educating the poor, bringing health to the primitive villages. These human ministries were apparent to non-Christian eyes. They carried a witness that did not need to be labored.

Today, in the villages in India, in the *barrios* of the Philippine Islands, in Japan, in Korea, in Africa, men are laboring for human welfare with, apparently, the same intensity that characterized the missionary. They are listening for hours to villagers to find out their needs, working patiently against superstition and disease, making plans for draining swamps and educating young minds.

Only a day or so ago I heard of a member of a United Nations team who, after explaining the aims of his team to an African village, was startled to have the headman say that he was willing to be baptized at once. The headman had never heard of a group interested in village welfare that was not a missionary group.

Another manifestation of revolution is the reformation and missionary zeal of many of the non-Christian religions. A missionary recently returned from India reported to his board on the *attractiveness* of reformed Hinduism to the young Indian. This group had attempted to meet some of the spiritual needs of the men and women round about. Some of its teachings had been taken over bodily from Christianity.

An American newspaperman has found reformed Buddhism so strong in its teachings of universal love among young Malayans of his acquaintance that he feels he has at last found "true Christian love." These facts change the pattern of the mission of the church as much as political facts change the pattern.

In the political field, where communism has already taken over the main thing one can do in missionary strategy is leave it to the Christians of the country. But in those countries where communism, or some other form of totalitarianism, *may* take over, those responsible for the mission of the church must prepare for what may come.

I once met with a group of Christian ministers in such a country. It was during the war. I had supposed they wanted me to talk about the United States and the war, and I worked quite hard to give them some picture of the church in the United States and the war. They were not interested. They had only one question to ask. They wanted to know if I had any knowledge of what other churches had done in countries like theirs. Was it possible to organize an underground church in such a way that faith lived on in the young?

At the Boston meeting of the Division of Foreign Missions of the National Council, there was a good deal of discussion, particularly among the Nationals, about the one who is to present the gospel in mission lands. In some areas a foreign missionary, particularly if he is Western, cannot evangelize through preaching. The national Christian, however, has a good deal of religious freedom in most mission lands. On him must fall some of the work carried in the past by the missionary. Judging by the national participants in Boston, he is eager and able to take over his share of the load.

There is, nevertheless, a load for the missionary. He is needed for his skills and he is needed as a witness to the interracial, ecumenical nature of the Christian church. This second need was mentioned by all Nationals at the meeting. Each time the emphasis was made it seemed to change a bit more the pattern of things to come. The concept of "sending-receiving countries" was dimmed by the concept of a world mission doing its planning on a global scale although there was a place for two country agreements. One must remember that this conference was considering things to come, not things already here. It may be some time before the concept mentioned above has flesh on its bones.

One other idea that emerged from the conference should be mentioned as contributing to a new pattern: the emphasis on the fact that the church lives in the world and the church must identify itself with that world, not only in its pain and distress, but also "in its real acts of love and justice."

The World Council of Churches recognized this need of identification in its report on the evangelizing church. It suggested that the non-Christians of the world are not to be approached "arrogantly," that we must remember that the Lord "did not leave himself without witness."

The papers, panels, and discussions in which these ideas appear make up the bulk of this book. They are taken from the written or spoken words of missionaries, both Western and Eastern, and of other leaders of the churches at home and overseas.

Some suggestions are given for cutting the pattern. In some instances only the fact of a need is declared. But it must be remembered that no pattern can be cut until a need is known.

DOROTHY McCONNELL

New York City
April, 1955

PATTERN OF THINGS TO COME

the beginning

of the pattern

by Dr. Peter Emmons

Jesus, thinking of the future, turned to his disciples and said, in effect, "I have made no other arrangements." Here is a tremendous truth. Because Jesus had made no other arrangements, the success of his divine enterprise for the salvation of a lost world was turned over to human instruments, and he knew it. And, therefore, he didn't just issue a general invitation and wait to see who would come. He didn't just start a movement or set up an organization and then begin a campaign for members. No. Jesus called unto himself those whom he desired and they came to him. He selected individuals and called each of them to an intimacy with himself, and they came, each of them, to him.

I am sure we have all thought of what a strange and almost impossible combination of human personalities there are here. There is Peter whom I know so well. And alongside of Peter there is Nathanael, that precise and proper individual of whom Jesus himself said, "Now there is a Hebrew without guile." There are James and John whom Jesus himself nicknamed "sons of thunder." What an insight into their character! And alongside of them Jesus put Judas—that cold, calculating individual, who was always looking for what he could "get out of it."

But I think the strangest combination of all is Simon Zelotes, or Simon the gorilla, the man who had signed up with the underworld of his day to plot against Rome and to be ready for the revolution. And alongside of him Jesus put Matthew, the publican, the man who had hired himself out to collect taxes from his own people to support the Roman

3

Empire. How could Jesus ever expect these men to stick together, much less to get along together and work together?

Well, you know the answer. He called them unto himself, and they came to him. And when they had come to him they found each other. That's the beginning, the only beginning, of the pattern of things to come.

Whatever we're going to plan, whatever we are going to hope for, whatever we are going to envision these days, here is where it begins. He called them to himself that they might be with him and be sent out to preach and to cast out demons. That is the whole pattern today—to preach and cast out demons.

You remember the story of the little old lady who was being shown through Westminster Abbey. It was one of the ambitions of her life to visit that historic place, and she had envisioned all the glory of the church at its best. A professional guide was showing her the places of historic interest. She stood it just as long as she could and finally she blurted out, "Young man! Young man! Will you stop your chatter for a minute and tell me—has anybody been saved here lately?" In Westminster Abbey? Why not? That's the church's business. No matter how the pattern is shaped, that's our business. And the business of the representatives of Jesus Christ is to bring men and women and boys and girls to know him, whom to know is life eternal.

Lord Jesus, Son of the Living God and Savior of all men, we come to thee with no pretense of personal adequacy but with a yearning to be with thee. Help us now to feel thy presence and in the hours to come, in fellowship with thyself, help us to face the challenge of thy divine mission in our world. Bless those of whom we are thinking and with whom we are associated in this divine mission all across the world. Be with thy children in every land, and may thy disciples of every race and nation,

4

in fellowship with thee, find unity of purpose and of spirit and a sense of task that may bind us together with ties of love that can never be broken. We pray in thine own name. Amen.

O Holy Saviour, Friend unseen,
    Since on Thine arm Thou bidd'st me lean,
Help me, throughout life's changing scene,
    By faith to cling to Thee.

—Charlotte Elliott

the pattern
of things to come
in evangelism

*In the discussion on evangelism Rolf A. Syrdal took up
the task of evangelism itself. He did not relate his words
to an area or a situation. He talked about what evangelism
is. His words were so final in meaning that they are included
here at some length.*

THE EVANGELISTIC TASK
by Rolf A. Syrdal

We cannot set the pattern of things to come in evangelism. The pattern has been set for us by God. It is for us
to find his pattern. We know that men are sunk in sin, that
the world needs a message to lift it up, and that in this
troubled world men need to be drawn into fellowship with
God. In the Old Testament we read how God reached out
and called men who went out with such assurance that when
they spoke they were able to say, "Thus saith the Lord
. . ." In the New Testament Jesus Christ, mingling among
men, called out a tax collector, or a fisherman, and said that
these were to be his witnesses unto the ends of the world.

In both these instances we find that these men were conscious both of the need of men and of the call of God. Man
is the messenger-servant, sometimes torn between looking
unto God and seeking to understand his command—that call
to serve—and looking unto mankind whom he is to serve in
pity and compassion, stirred with human pity and patiently
trusting in divine compassion to direct him into the ways in
which he should walk.

In our day, we look upon a world where even the stable
governments seem to have their next move planned for them
in advance by political influences and military powers. We
have sometimes trembled, wondering what we are to do,
what is the change that must take place. As we look into
the future we realize that there is one thing that must remain—the clear message of God. Our words must be an
answer to the deepest needs of man. It becomes vital that
our words be effective for our age.

First of all, our evangelism must be a proclamation. I think that, of all the messages that were given at the time of Jesus Christ by those who had found him, there is one that stands out in its simple eloquence. The man who gave it was a man of few words. Our Lord had healed him, and when asked how it was that Jesus of Nazareth could do such things, he said, "One thing I know, that though I was blind, now I see." This is the proclamation.

Then there is the church, a place of divine fellowship with man and God. We know that the Holy Spirit lives within the church. Under persecution we have seen the church emerging with a message that has been so forceful that we, who have not suffered, have had to kneel in shame because we have been so lukewarm in comparison.

We speak of the deeds of love. The ministry of healing, the schools, the agricultural programs, and other allied forms of social service are a pure manifestation of God's love. These deeds come out of a heart that is filled with love. Our Lord said, "As you did it to one of the least of these my brethren, you did it to me." Still we dare not omit the spoken message of the dying and risen Savior lest we give only things of lesser value and leave out that which is of utmost value—the saving of the individual and the creation of a right spirit, a re-birth in Christ. That is the regeneration that we ultimately seek.

In our day we do seek conversion. We do seek to establish brotherhood with others in every sphere, in every geographic area. God's call to us has not been rescinded, nor has it been changed. We meet the conditions of our world today in eternal confidence. When one door closes we use another. When one phase ends we begin another. When one way ceases to be available to us we go another way, pliable in methods, but firm in our mission and final goal.

8

Discussion

The papers and discussion that followed Dr. Syrdal's presentation showed a variety of emphases. But they had one common element. Each of those who spoke on evangelism in some particular country spoke of the atmosphere of desire for responsibility in that country.

"Formerly," said Dr. Bhandare of India, "evangelism through medicine, education, or land improvement was carried on by the missionary and Christian helpers. Today the non-Christians say, '*We* will educate, *we* will heal, *we* will improve the land.'"

How, he asks, does one unite with the non-Christian in services and still proclaim the gospel through acts of love? He does not attempt to answer the question. He asks that ways be studied to find the answers. He is also disturbed by the large numbers of his countrymen who insist that industrialization is the one answer to India's problem. It leaves the emphasis on spiritual values, once a very great concern of even non-Christian Indians, in the hands of the Christians. But how does one make such an emphasis, worn smooth by use, effective in a country newly aroused to industry?

There are two facts that give Dr. Bhandare hope in his complex task. One is that the growing move toward unity may result in a church of India, able to speak for the Lord in a combined voice. The other is that the illiterate Christian, often a worker in the field or factory, is being taught to speak for the Lord to the non-Christian in the row, or on the bench, next to him.

Mr. John Kaemmer of Southeast Africa spoke of the growing desire for responsibility among the people with whom he works.

"The older people who have been converted like to hear preaching," he said, "just preaching. They can't seem to get enough of it. But the young people are bored with preaching."

The proclamation must come to them, Mr. Kaemmer thinks, through their own creative experience. Music can have an evangelistic value. Camps and conferences where all who participate can widen horizons and change lives. Dramas may carry deep

9

currents of emotional feeling that have powerful effects on African hearts.

As Mr. Kaemmer suggested methods of evangelization he fell back into the thought that, however fine the methods used, Christianity is, after all, the whole of life and the gospel must be presented "by our actions as well as by our words."

Dr. Carl Kriete, formerly a missionary in Japan, comes from a country where the church has governed itself for some time. The people are highly literate. But there is need to help the literate, self-governing church of Japan in the evangelistic task.

The Christian schools are, he feels, perhaps the best places for nurture in the Christian life. From the schools there should be an out-thrust into the non-Christian world. Every day Japanese bookstalls are crowded, after classes, with young non-Christian university students looking for something to read. Here is the challenge, a challenge that scholars in the Christian schools (and the International Christian University) can answer if they are encouraged.

There was considerable discussion from the audience after the papers were read. The question came up again, as it did in one way or another throughout the conference, of the place of the non-Christian man of good will who was friendly to Christianity, but did not become a part of it. Gandhi was the great example, Gandhi who used the gospel every day in his devotions.

"What was Gandhi's influence on the Christian movement?" someone asked.

Dr. Bhandare answered that his influence was favorable to the missionary. His regard for Christianity had the opposite effect. His adaptation of Christianity to his own uses cost it, in the eyes of the people about him, its unique difference.

Perhaps Mr. C. I. Itty of India suggested one of the newest approaches to evangelism, as well as a way of working together. We include his presentation here for that reason. A summary of the new pattern as it emerges in Indonesia appears at the end of the presentation.

INDONESIAN VENTURE
by C. I. Itty

Today we have a concern about the new patterns that are shaping up in evangelistic and missionary enterprises. This concern is a concern of the church throughout the world. The churches that I represent, the churches of Southeast Asia, have an equal concern with the churches of the West, and a deep awareness of the new pattern that we have to shape in evangelistic work in the future.

The age-old missionary era has come to an end, and a new ecumenical era is on the way to being born. The awareness of the new era brings with it a new responsibility to us of Southeast Asia. The so-called younger churches are aware of a responsibility for evangelism in their own lands and the lands adjoining them.

Today you will find that there are Indian missionaries working in southern parts of Africa, in Ethiopia, in Nepal, in Indonesia, in Australia and New Guinea. I am one of the fortunate ones to be called by the Indonesian church and fortunate to be sent by the Indian church. This is a new pattern.

I want to mention a few points that suggest something about the pattern that we have to shape in the future.

First of all, I went to Indonesia because the Indonesian church invited me. It is they who made the choice and they who made the decision. It was in 1950 that I went to Indonesia for the first time in connection with two of our conferences on the work of our Christian Federation. When I returned to India I had an invitation from the Board of the National Council of Churches in Indonesia and the

Board of the Christian Student Movement in Indonesia, to return to Indonesia at least for a period of one year to work for them. They made the choice and they made the decision. I had only to respond.

Secondly, though the church in Indonesia called me, it was the church in India that sent me. The church in India was already beginning to feel the labor pains of a new ecumenical era. When it heard about the invitation from Indonesia for me to go there and to work, it was glad to give me a good send-off. Several meetings were held throughout South India and Travancore where people came together to show their concern for the new evangelistic enterprises and the movement that was on its way. When I left the harbor of Colombo for Indonesia I felt that half the work was already done—not in Indonesia, but in my own country, India, to make it realize its part in evangelism throughout the world.

Thirdly, it was not really an affair between the church in India and the church in Indonesia; it was a corporate ecumenical uplift and a symbol of the whole world church united. For example, who paid for my travel? It was not the Indian church nor the Indonesian church. When the news of my invitation went to Geneva and to Amsterdam, immediately the church in Holland was willing to pay the travel expenses and even booked the seat in the plane. It was ecumenical in the sense that it was not merely the pooling of Dutch guilders, it was also the pooling of Dutch guilders with Indonesian rupees and Indian rupees. For example, when I went to Indonesia I was asked to go empty-handed. When I left Indonesia I left empty-handed, too, because I wanted it to be so. I was paid by an Indonesian church just like any other Indonesian worker in the church, and I left without taking a single cent to any other country.

But when I landed back in Madras, I received a letter from the National Council of the Y.M.C.A. in India, saying, "Mr. Itty: We are very glad to inform you that a gift of a substantial amount of money is waiting for you as a token of the happy feeling toward your work in Indonesia." I had worked for the Y.M.C.A. only one year. But that letter shows that without any appeal, without anybody's asking, the church feels its responsibility and expresses itself through its different forms.

The experience was ecumenical in many respects. I belong to the Syrian Orthodox Church, which is not even Protestant. The church where I worked in Indonesia was in the Presbyterian tradition. In their missionary concern my own church, conservative as it is, was prepared to give me, to lend my services for a church that is of a different division, of different dogma and different theological background. And when I went to Indonesia, they in Indonesia were not afraid of my heresies, traditions, isms, and other things that were in me. We were united so that the world may believe.

One result of my two-and-a-half years of work was within the church in Indonesia. First, the place of Indians as missionaries was accepted in all the churches of Indonesia. Before I left I had the great pleasure of working with a Philippine couple who had been called to Indonesia. It was another example of the use of missionary personnel from the Asian countries.

The National Council in India has had a request from the Indonesian church for more than a dozen Indian missionaries to work in Indonesia immediately. A plan is on its way for its materialization. This is a great achievement, not merely in the fact of getting more missionary personnel in the field, but also in the fact of real missionary concern in the two churches. For example, the Indian church was challenged several times by expressions and reflections that I carried back from my experience in the Indonesian church. The evangelistic fervor, for instance, of the Indonesian church was a great critique of the Indian church.

At the same time, the Indonesian church was able to secure new insights into a new technique of evangelism that we in India had, which they in Indonesia did not know. The different traditions and different backgrounds contributed to each other and complemented each other in our evangelistic work.

I want to mention two more points. They come from experiences that I had while I was in Indonesia. One was an experience of international teamwork in the matter of evangelism. I had the privilege on several occasions, and in several stages in my work in Indonesia, to work in cooperation—close cooperation—with fellow missionaries from Australia, from the United States, from Holland, from Switzerland, from the Philippines, and from Germany. These six or seven nationalities represented the Christian gospel in a unified way. We worked at one place and at one project on several occasions, and there we realized how different we are, and at the same time what a unique place everybody has. In arranging a conference nobody can equal the planning and the organization of an American. But at the same time there is no one like an Australian in keeping accounts. And we, the Asians from the Philippines and India, we could meet the people in the villages without any difficulties because we had the advantage of color.

We felt, as we worked on those projects together, that here is the world church in action for evangelism. And then we began to question our traditions of one denomination and one nation monopolizing the work of another area.

Another experience that I had was in the matter of lay missionary work. While I was working in Indonesia I had the opportunity to come in contact with the Australian Student Christian Movement in the sending of graduate students from Australia to Indonesia. The Australian Student Christian Movement recruited graduates in engineering and medicine, and in such similar subjects. They were recruited because they were missionary-minded personnel. They were sent to Indonesia to work in the Indonesian government, getting authority from the Indonesian government. They were making their spirit and faith contagious, and their impact was tremendous within the country and among the young people in Indonesia. More than five young people have worked for the past two years. More are coming. The team, I may say, is appreciated by the government as well as by the Christians. It made me aware of the fact that we may have to question the efficiency of having so-called full time Christian workers labeled as missionaries in these non-Christian areas with secular governments, and that we ought to penetrate and permeate such areas outside the church. We ought not to borrow foreign missionaries for lay work, as such, in the American embassies, or the American Information Service, or TCA and other fields. Maybe we should employ some of our missionary-minded persons for these jobs.

The churches in Southeast Asia are conscious of a new pattern. We are weak, there is no doubt about that, but we are enabled to be strong by His grace and your cooperation. We are sure that we are together with the one great world-wide church. We intend to go forward in the great enterprise of evangelism developing new patterns and at the same time renewing the old patterns with our unfaltering faith in Him.

A NEW PATTERN OF MISSIONARY EVANGELISM IN INDONESIA

The church of Indonesia asked for the services of Mr. Itty (by name) of the church of India.

Mr. Itty, a Syrian Orthodox, was asked to serve in the Indonesian church, a church of Presbyterian theological background.

The Dutch Reformed Church of Holland paid his plane fare.

The Y.M.C.A. deposited money, when he returned from Indonesia, for expenses when he first arrived in India.

The church in Indonesia paid his salary during the time he was on Indonesian soil.

RESULTS OF THE PATTERN

Asian missionaries began to be accepted as "natural" in Indonesia.

The request from Indonesia for Indian missionaries became the stimulus for concentrated attention by Indians on missionary opportunity.

Indian and Indonesian techniques were interchanged.

The Western missionaries and the Asian had the experience of working together as an ecumenical team.

THOUGHT PROVOKERS

1. Can you see how such a pattern of evangelism as Mr. Itty speaks of here can be worked in churches having dissimilar theological backgrounds?

2. Does Mr. Syrdal have help for us here?

3. What does Mr. Syrdal mean when he says all evangelism must be a proclamation?

4. Do you think this proclamation helps in meeting the desire to show how Christianity is unique?

5. Can you think of ways by which Christians can unite with non-Christians in "acts of love"?

6. What is the advantage of a united church in the Asian world in the evangelistic task?

16

7. Can you think of a way, perhaps suggested in this section, of how Christians can bring the religious emphasis in industry—particularly in a country newly aroused to industry?

8. Do you think that lay evangelism should be a major consideration of mission strategy?

9. What do you think of Mr. Itty's suggestion that missionary-minded lay people be used for work in embassies, technical assistance teams, and other fields?

10. Do you feel that the Christian mission school is still the best place for the nurture of Christian life?

the pattern
of things to come
in southern asia

*Dr. Moses' paper was given early in the conference.
In itself it set a pattern of thinking throughout the
conference. Members of the body rose and asked that the
speech be reprinted in full in these pages. There have
been some editorial cuts. There have been no cuts that
change the thesis of the paper, none that delete any of the
points that he developed as part of that thesis.
A summary of Dr. Moses' plan to shape
the pattern appears at the end of this section.*

by David G. Moses

There is something of a suggestion that the pattern of things to come in Southern Asia will be a natural evolution, the inevitable resultant of the new forces that are operating in that area. I am convinced that this implication is erroneous. The pattern of things to come will have to be brought about by much consecrated thinking and earnest prayer. It will be the result of a creative evolution; it will be a novel emergent, connected indeed with the patterns of the past and influenced by the changed conditions operating there, but essentially something novel.

Even as the pattern of things to come in Southern Asia is not something that will emerge by itself, this pattern will not be arbitrary. It will be in a real sense a pattern shaped after a permanent purpose.

Therefore it is necessary to remind ourselves of the twin foundations of Christian missions, the gospel of Jesus Christ and the church. The gospel is the good news that in the fullness of time God entered the scene of human history in the person of Jesus Christ to transform it into the theatre of his glory. It is the entrance of a new power to break down walls of partition, to bring peace to them that were afar off and to them that were near. This gospel the church has been commissioned to declare.

Church and Mission Are One

In all the countries of Southern Asia the church's activities have been based on a radical distinction between the church and the mission. In the consciousness of the ordinary Christian, the church is one thing and the mission is quite another. To some extent he feels responsible to the church, but the mission of the church he delegates to the paid evangelists and the missionaries. This situation is rapidly changing and increasing numbers of Christians are beginning to realize that the church is the mission and that the very *raison d'être* of the church is the mission. All our efforts must be concentrated to abolish this distinction, which has taken such a deep root.

It will mean the following deliberately taken steps:

1. We must proceed with greater haste and increasing thoroughness toward the policy of integration of church and mission so happily begun in so many missions in Southern Asia.

2. We must make provision that a church formed by any group of believers becomes the mission and insist that the individual Christian does not exist as a Christian unless he is also a missionary Christian.

3. We must develop and train leadership for Christian witnessing from the very beginning.

4. We must express the principle that all our works, however varied they may be, should be judged by the overriding importance of the church's mission.

Mission in Unity

There is a growingly recognized principle that missions are missions only as they are in unity. The words of the Lord of the church are quite clear. He prayed, "That they may all be one; even as thou, Father, art in me . . . that the world may believe that thou hast sent me."

This new pattern of united churches engaged in the united task of missions is already emerging in Southern Asia. In a few years' time it will become the dominant and universal pattern. Missions and churches should devote all their efforts to bring about this consummation, because the mission of the church cannot otherwise be fulfilled.

The curses of the countries of Southern Asia, and especially India, have been disunity, division, and middle walls of partition. If this new pattern of things to come is to emerge in Southern Asia, it will call upon the churches of the participating countries for deep heart-searchings and new efforts toward expressing the oneness we have in Christ.

The Christian Church Is Ecumenical

One feature in the new pattern that we must take care to preserve is the ecumenical character of the church. It is so easy in the countries of Southern Asia, especially in India and Ceylon and Burma, for the Christian church to mold itself after the pattern of a national or sectarian church. The Hindu does not know, and we Christians have not helped him to know, that the church is a supra-national and supra-racial society, and that the task of the church can never be properly fulfilled except in the united witness of different Nationals. Even when the churches of Southern Asia are fully self-supporting, and can manage all their activities, it will still be necessary to have in their fellowship believers from other lands and other races to be partners in obedience to the commission of our Lord. The churches in Southern Asia should never cease to present to their non-Christian countrymen evidence in actual living of the ecumenical character of the Christian faith.

The Church Has Indigenous Character

Still another prominent feature of the new pattern of things to come in Southern Asia will be the genuinely indigenous character of the church in every one of the lands of

Southern Asia. A characteristic of most of the churches in Southern Asia is their pronounced foreign-ness.

The great hymn of Isaac Watts sings of bringing peculiar honors to our King. But when we look at our churches in this region, barring a few notable exceptions, they are all pale and anemic imitations of the churches of the West. Of course, we must be aware of the dangers that beset this task. In India, surrounded by a religion whose genius is to absorb and assimilate and to kill another faith by a fraternal embrace, there is, of course, the great danger of losing the unique nature of our faith.

The cultural heritage of India is Christ's, and we must make the valid elements in it captive to our Lord and Master. Our churches in South India, especially, have taken the music of India and made it captive to the Lord of the church. When converts from the higher castes, in the early days, came to Jesus with their rich religious heritage they poured their experiences of new deliverance in Christ back into the poetry and music of the land of their birth. The tendency in recent decades has been to concentrate on the lower classes of Hindu society because they have been readily responsive to the liberating gospel of Jesus Christ. While we should have done this, we should not have left undone the duty of special approach to the educated and the higher castes who have the heritage of the country's culture. Today in all the countries of Southern Asia special opportunities are presenting themselves for a new witness to the Christian faith among the educated.

The Printed Word

In councils and conferences we have talked *ad lib* about newspaper evangelism, tracts for the times, and so on, but nothing much has been done. The Christian church has a great opportunity to witness to the growing number of educated people who see no purpose in life. The church can witness to the purposefulness of life rooted in the purposes of God and the sure hope of their final fulfillment. Today is also the opportune time for the church in all these countries that have chosen the democratic form of government to make a double witness by means of tracts for the times, to show the real roots of democracy in the Christian doctrine of man and, at the same time, the hollowness of men's hopes if they are to be centered in a particular form of government.

The Study of Old, Established Religions

There is also another important practical step that urgently needs to be taken if this new pattern of a genuinely indigenous church is to arise in the countries of Southern Asia. This is to stimulate scholarly study of the old, established religions of Hinduism, Buddhism, and Islam. In recent years, with the coming of independence and the powerful influence of nationalistic sentiments, there has been a religious renaissance. There is a tremendous intellectual activity in reformulating ancient doctrines in the light of new conditions. Doctrines that were inimical to human welfare, doctrines that sanctioned inequality and injustices, are relegated to the background and ignored, and ideas that are world-affirming and helpful in building a new society brought to the foreground. The claim is made that the dawn of a new day in Southern Asia is also the time for taking the ancient messages of their religions to what is called the spiritually benighted world of the West. Hindu culture claims today not only a place of equal validity with other views of life, but also a place of preeminence among the religions of the world. There is an exhilarating feeling among a growing number of people that India has entered a new era of mission to the world, and that it is her duty to proclaim to the world her message of truth and *ahisma* (non-violence).

Christians need to thank God for all this purification and weeding out of ancient superstitions that have come about in the non-Christian religions. And there is no need to fear that this all-embracing power of absorption of the Eastern religions can blur the distinctive characteristics of the Christian faith and appear identical with it. For only ideas are absorbed by other religions. The Christian faith is centered in a person, in Jesus Christ. The cross is not a beautiful idea; it is a stark existential reality. What is of serious concern for us is the fact that the task of apologetics has now become practically relegated to the background. Time was when authoritative scholars in the religions of Southern Asia were Christians. A virile and ongoing Christian apologetic was the result. Today the whole task of apologetics has come to a standstill.

The cross of Christ needs to be lifted up in the light of the Hindu and Buddhist reformulation of their own faith and in connection with the new movements that are springing up within Hinduism. The spiritually satisfying, genuinely indigenous church will not emerge until the gospel is preached in terms of the rich religious heritage of India, taking the age-old concepts, re-minting them with new content by the fire of the gospel, and using them as current coins of communication.

An Adequate Ministry

The new pattern of things that will emerge in Southern Asia will exemplify a radically revised organization and training of the ministry in the churches of this region. An adequate ministry is a crying need of India. Dr. Rajah

Manikam, in his book *Christianity and the Asian Revolution*, points out that "in India there are approximately 11,000 organized congregations and about 9,000 unorganized groups of Protestant Christians; to minister to these there are only 3,000 ordained ministers, national and foreign."

In the past we have transplanted the Western conception of a Christian ministry to the East where the conditions are very different. A full-time, paid ministry has been the norm, but on this basis it is impossible to provide a ministry adequate to the needs of multiplying congregations as a result of group movements. The result has been not only that congregations have been starved of their necessary spiritual food, but they have existed as less than real churches of God. Bishop Lesslie Newbigin says, "In the New Testament the local congregation is treated as the church of God in that place. It is not a branch of an organization; it *is* God's gathering in that place. Moreover, it is a church furnished with a ministry of 'all the Saints in Christ Jesus . . . with the Bishops and Deacons.' The New Testament knows nothing of a church without a ministry."

When an itinerant minister is responsible for ten, twenty, thirty, and even sixty village congregations, these churches never know an outgoing life of evangelistic ministry. Mission boards and churches should seriously consider whether this whole pattern is not wrong, whether the churches themselves, from the very beginning, should not become responsible for its ministry and whether we should not boldly experiment with a part-time ordained ministry.

The World Mission of the Church

So far missions have been mainly denominational. They have served their purpose admirably under the hand of God. But times have changed. The great new fact of our era is

the world church. It is no longer possible to make the old distinction between the sending churches and receiving churches. There is a new missionary enthusiasm among the so-called younger churches, and they have already begun to send men and women from their churches to other lands, to work among other people. The present disturbed international situation makes it impossible for missionaries from some nations to go to their fellow Christians in other nations. This need not mean the cutting off of all ecumenical contact with some churches, for Christians from nations that are politically friendly could go to them and keep alive the Christian unity. But, it must be borne in mind, this new pattern is needed not to meet the exigencies of a disturbed political situation; it is called for by our new understanding of the task of the church. It is nothing less than the world mission and it can be undertaken only by a world missionary society, transcending all denominational, national, and congregational differences. It will mean a pooling of all our resources as a world church and the most complete partnership in obedience that has ever been the characteristic of our missionary undertaking.

The Church Is in the World

In all our work to help shape a new pattern of things in Southern Asia, which will be more in consonance with the gospel of Jesus Christ and more in conformity with his mind, one overriding consideration should not be forgotten. All our work must be expressive of our deep identification with the needs of our world. Under the section, "The Missionary Calling of the Church," the Willingen Report says, "The church is in the world and as the Lord of the church identifies himself wholly with mankind, so must the church also do. . . . Christians do not live in an enclave in the world. Therefore the church is required to identify itself with the world, not only in its perplexity and distress, its guilt and its sorrow, but also in its real acts of love and justice."

The churches in India, Pakistan, Ceylon, and Burma are called to a far deeper identification with the people of their lands, especially at this time when in every one of those lands efforts, private and governmental, are being made to right wrong, to abolish injustices, and to make possible a more abundant life for the citizens. The Christian faith expresses itself in the Christian hope that the redemption of history is from beyond history. It is built on the conviction that our God is a worker and that he is in the world working out his purposes. He can make the wrath of men praise him and he will, in the magnanimity of his grace, use our deeds of hope for his eternal glory. It is only as the church identifies herself with her land and its people with the same intensity of compassion and pardoning grace that the crucified Lord had in identifying himself with the world that we can ever hope to show them the light we have received.

NOTE: The unabridged speech may be had by writing to the Division of Foreign Missions, National Council of Churches, 156 Fifth Avenue, New York 10, N. Y.

OUTLINE OF THE PATTERN AS DR. MOSES SEES IT IN SOUTHERN ASIA

Church and mission will become one.

This "one" is a united body of what used to be denominations.

The united body will recognize its missionary task by sending workers abroad as well as working at home.

The united body will be the church of Southern Asia, but also part of the world church and above national and racial lines.

The united church will be indigenous—partly so it can best serve its community, partly so it can bring its own "peculiar honors" to the church as a whole.

Although the united church is indigenous it has a place for workers from other lands, if for no other reason than to testify to the world nature of the church.

The church will be part of the world around it as never before. To achieve this pattern the strategy is:

To make concentrated effort to abolish distinctions between church and mission.

To instruct new believers in becoming missionary Christians.

To train leadership to witness for Christianity from the very beginning.

To train more ministers.

To look at all Christian work in relation to its place in the mission of the church.

To seek every possible way to show the non-racial, non-national character of Christianity.

To work toward capturing the valid elements in Asian culture for the praise of the Lord.

To seek in all ways to bring into being the united church.

To promote the study of the Asian religions as they exist today.

To train ministers and new Christians in the unique difference to be found in Christianity.

To work out ways to make the church a part of the world around it.

THOUGHT PROVOKERS

1. What does Dr. Moses mean when he says the church is the mission—the mission the reason for the church?

2. How do you interpret the statement that the works or institutions of the church should be judged by the importance of the world's mission?

3. Do you feel that Dr. Moses is justified in his assertion that the mission of the church cannot be fulfilled except as the

churches are united somewhat after the pattern of the United Church of South India?

4. Is there anything inconsistent with the insistence on a genuinely indigenous church for Southern India with the concept of church as a supra-national, supra-racial divine fellowship?

5. Why do Hindu, Buddhist, and Islamic religions need to be studied anew?

6. Do you agree with the concept of a local congregation as "the church of God in that place" and that the New Testament did not know a congregation without a ministry?

7. How can you erase the distinction between "sending" and "receiving" churches and still promote missions?

8. What does the author mean when he says the church is required to identify itself with the world "in its real acts of love and justice"?

There have always been heated discussions on the role of the institution on a mission field. The new factor is that such discussions are given major importance.

In Boston one heard constant discussions—in corridors, in lunchrooms, before meetings began.

One person said, "The school in my area is doing one of the best pieces of witnessing in the whole country. But the church, and the mission, is always 'after it.' It keeps its standards high and will not lower them for anyone. But that is part of the trouble. Our Christian children coming from the rural countryside cannot make the grade. Their places are filled by the city-bred non-Christians."

Another person—"I remember the trouble we had years ago when one of our missionaries opened a prayer room in the school for Muslims. Years later Mr. Birge, one of the famous missionaries of Istanbul, said he thought that prayer room was one of the finest services the school had ever given to the country."

Still another said, "But shouldn't the Christian institutions give first attention to the Christians? Isn't that what they are for?"

In the atmosphere of these questions, many of them by puzzled administrators of institutions, Dr. Alford Carleton spoke.

by Alford Carleton

In considering the pattern of things to come in our institutions, it would seem at first glance, with the growth of the younger churches, that the obvious thing is to turn all mission institutions over to the local church authorities. It would then be their task to work out the problem of balance and perspective of the institution to the total Christian effort in an area. Actually it is by no means that simple. The care of the funds, or the rivalry for the power of caring for them, or the jealousy that can surround appointments and positions of influence in the schools and hospitals, may be a greater strain upon the life of a young church than would be the case were the institutions not in their care at all.

Similarly, it must be carefully evaluated whether the school and hospital exist fundamentally for the service of the existing church and the Christian community or whether they have been established largely as means of outreach and evangelism toward the surrounding non-Christian communities. In the former case it is easy for the church to operate them in scale and proportion to their own resources and work. In the other case it may be very difficult indeed. A college with a majority of non-Christians on the staff, or in the student body, may prove far more a liability than an asset to the church that is given its control. It may even be considered that there is a place for the deliberately foreign school or hospital to continue to do certain things for the community outside the church, in order to accomplish certain purposes without putting the burden of responsibility upon the local church community. That is, admittedly, an exception and to be considered only under unusual circumstances.

The best approach is to evaluate the needs, the strength, the possibilities of the Christian community, and *only then* to consider what is to be done with the institutions that have already been built up in that same area. Perhaps the church should have schools and hospitals, and yet it might be possible that the schools and hospitals now in existence and in the hands of the missions, or of joint mission and church committees, are not right in size, type, or organization to be put directly into the control of the churches. Is the budget so big as to overbalance the work of the church? Should the work be cut down before it is turned over? Is it possible that it should continue independently for some time? Such questions need to be asked with care.

It is quite possible that, if the local church community cannot carry the larger units of institutional work, it may be better to internationalize them. In that way the institution comes under the Christians of the different areas of the world. Certainly priority should be given to the Christians on the spot and yet strict nationalization is against the universal genius of Christian faith. In that connection there is great hope in the ecumenical mission. "International" does not have to mean either "white" or "Western."

Meanwhile, experience with institutions has shown that there are many practical ways of maintaining their spiritual impact and relating them continuously to the Christian enterprise as a whole. If I speak of schools, that is because my own experience lies in that field. The same principles are applicable to all types of institutions.

The first is that the staff, from the janitor to the principal, be worthy examples of Christian faith and conduct.

Under circumstances where the whole clientele of the school is Christian, it is reasonable that all employees of the institution be practicing members of the church. Where there are reasons for the employment of non-Christian staff, they should be in a minority and very carefully chosen for character standards and for an attitude of comprehension and tolerance toward the school and the community it represents. The larger the proportion of non-Christians in the student body, or the higher the degree of legal restriction on religious instruction, the more significant is the standard of Christian life and teaching implicit in the character of the staff of the institution.

The second principle is that the professional level of the institution, the ethical standards of treatment of its own staff, and its reputation for scrupulous observance of the law of the land and the regulations of the department of education be such as to command respect. Nothing will so quickly reduce a school from an effective agency of evangelism to a mere center of proselytism (using the terms as our critics might) as will the impression that it is a cloak for professional propaganda and not a self-respecting institution in its own right.

The third principle is that the religious instruction and the services of worship of the institution be, so far as the law permits, integrated into the totality of the life of the institution, and not set apart as special exercises in piety. Whether "conversion" be taken as renewal of life on the part of a member of the Christian community, or as a radical change of faith on the part of a non-Christian, it is rarely the direct result of participation in a Bible class or in a service of corporate worship. When that moment of readiness is reached, however, perhaps from an experience on the playground or an unexpected act of forgiveness on the part of a teacher, the clarification of the classroom or the fellowship of the worship service become invaluable means of grace. The balance of the religious and the secular aspect of the life of a school should keep the one from drifting into mere pietism and the other from settling into mere secularism.

Underlying these three principles there is the need of constant watchfulness, thoughtfulness, and imagination. Habit, inertia, routine, and the spiritual drowsiness brought on by too much care for petty concerns will turn any school from a creditable Christian institution into an institution-alized treadmill, no better than its non-Christian counter-parts and with far less material resources.

The final principle in considering the pattern of things to come in our institutions is that we must hold all things in a light grasp. We must be open to the leading of God as to the forms, the organization, the administration, and the leadership of any institution that we set up. We must make sure that it is ever moving forward to serve the purpose for which it was established and that it is not merely institutionalized. We must make sure that it takes its place in the total Christian enterprise. In the end that depends upon the men and women who serve it, who lead it, and who control it. A great responsibility lies therefore upon not only the local congregations and the local boards of managers and trustees, but also upon those who over the world determine the major policies and distribution of resources of the Christian movement as a whole.

THOUGHT PROVOKERS

1. What conditions should be met before a Christian institution is turned over to the Christian church of the country?

2. Where the Christian church is not strong enough to take

over the institution, how can the stigma of foreign control be avoided?

3. Can you think of situations where the institution may be carried on independently outside the church?

4. Do you think a Christian institution can witness without Bible teaching (for instance) or compulsory worship?

5. Is there a place for a non-Christian on the institution staff? If you decide there is, what should be the guide for choosing him?

6. Do you feel that the standards themselves of a hospital or school can effect a witness?

7. What do you feel the author means by holding "all things in a light grasp"?

the pattern
of things to come
in africa

Some time ago "Life" magazine gave over an entire issue to pictures and articles on Africa. It followed the "Saturday Review," which had just had a number dealing with African books. In the wake of these came articles in the country's leading journals. The articles and books dealt with two facts— Africa's emerging significance as an industrial country and Africa's race problem.

These two facts affect every part of Africa south of the Sahara. They have an effect on every part of the civilized world. They are the two facts that challenge the mission strategy. They are the two facts that were talked about generally before and after the paper by Dr. Carpenter.
One missionary in a private discussion said that the tribe with whom he worked went to the nearby city just to look at the lights. He said that the lights were bewitching the African.

Another said it was economic necessity that drove the African to the city. "But," he added, "once he had had the city experience the old tribal village loses its appeal."

Most earnest discussions centered around the question, How can you build a Christian community where there is racial discrimination?

"How do you tell the story of love," said one, "in a city where an African does not cross a park because Christians have drawn up restrictions against Africans entering a park gate?"

Again and again there was hope expressed that the conflict could be resolved by the World Council of Churches working within the Christian church.

by George W. Carpenter

There is a familiar African story about a traveler on safari who found one morning that his carriers refused to leave camp. When he asked the reason, they replied, "We have come so far so very fast that we must give our souls time to catch up with us."

It would be a blessing if Africa could have a day, or a year, or perhaps a century of repose in which her soul might catch up with her body. But the pace of change is inexorably swift.

The Price of Progress

Two weeks ago today I was in the office of the acting governor of a province of the South Sudan. Outside, amid the clatter of a busy river port on the Nile, one could see naked tribesmen from the hinterlands striding up and down, with their matted hair bleached red with cowdung ashes. Inside, the governor (a Sudanese, a Muslim, a university graduate) talked with us about mission-government relationships and how we can best cooperate in the interests of those people.

Just south of the town a large agricultural experiment station has been set up because it is proposed to dig a canal to regulate the flow of the Nile. When that is done the flat plains of South Sudan will no longer be flooded every year. Much of the pasturage used by those tribes will become arid, and they will have to depend on crops instead of cattle for their livelihood.

In the gold-mining area of the Midwaters Rand at least

a million Africans are employed, recruited from all over southern Africa. The vast majority are there without their wives, living in bed spaces in overcrowded barracks, or perhaps in rented shacks in the most casual and temporary relations with a succession of women. Not until these men approach middle age and settle in their villages for good, after long years in the mines, will many of them be able to enjoy family life in any true sense. In many tribes a contract on the Rand has taken the place of the old tribal initiation rite. It is the way a boy becomes a man. Everybody goes to the Rand—all of the men and many of the girls. It is quite unrealistic to suppose either that African society can be reconstituted or that a vital Christian church can take root as long as this vicious system continues to prevail.

Moving with the Tide

There is, of course, a sound alternative. Through many years' experience in the Congo, and more recently in other territories, it has been demonstrated that when wives and children are brought with the men to industrial centers, when decent homes are made available and living wages are paid, then a stable, happy, and increasingly skillful and prosperous urban community can be built up. Recruiting becomes unnecessary. Migration is reduced to a minimum. And the villages also thrive because the young men are not continually going away and coming back. With reasonably stable populations both city and country churches can grow strong, develop an adequate ministry, and exert a powerful influence for moral wholesome living. This better way is also cheaper in the end because the human and economic waste of migrancy is avoided and the capacities of the workers are more fully realized.

The African does not go to the mine or seek other industrial employment for the pleasure of it. There may be adventure, but fundamentally he is driven by sheer economic necessity. In many places his numbers are too great to live on the land that is left to him, impoverished as it often is by overgrazing, faulty cultivation, and erosion. His wants have multiplied as commerce has brought European wares within his reach.

Not least, he wants education for his children so that they may take their place more effectively in the new Africa he sees opening before him. To this end he will make great sacrifices. Yet often, when he tries to advance in European culture and economy, into which he is being thrust, the African finds himself thwarted by cruel barriers of race discrimination.

Lord, Who Is My Brother?

The cultural differences between the tribesmen and the European formed a natural line of separation in the beginning. The critical choice today is whether that separation is to be enforced by rigid permanent barriers based on race, or whether the differences of culture are to be progressively overcome in the interests of national unity and self-realization.

The South African Government, in a sincere but misguided belief that separation must be maintained, a policy that is unhappily based to some extent on the Hebrew nationalism of the Old Testament, is moving steadily toward greater rigidity and increasingly burdensome restrictions on freedom for all of its people. I talked with African leaders who were quite unable to believe that the leaders of the government are sincere in the policies that they impose. And yet if you talk with the men in the government you can have no doubt at all that they are not only sincere, but are idealists.

Farther north, in the new Federation of Rhodesia Nyasaland, there is a definite movement toward the creation of a multi-racial society. Nobody can foresee just yet what the form of such a society must be, but many of the best minds and finest spirits among all races are being mobilized to meet and solve the issue.

The gravity of this issue is thrown into relief by the Mau Mau in Kenya. Mau Mau started as a terrorists' secret society of the Kikuyu people. The Kikuyu are one of the great tribes of Kenya. They number about a million people, and constitute about one-fifth of the population of the country. Mau Mau was dedicated to the aim of driving the Europeans out of Kenya. Its leaders hoped to enlist the entire tribe, and began to use intimidation and torture to force tribesmen to take its oaths in a series of unspeakably vile and revolting ceremonies. Christian Kikuyu, especially those related to the great Eastern African Christian revival, resisted and denounced the movement with the result that they have borne the brunt of its violence. More than five hundred of them have been killed, as against about fifty of the Europeans against whom the movement was supposedly directed. Suppression of the movement has cost another thousand or more lives, and some fifty thousand Kikuyus are in detention camps behind barbed wire at this moment.

Rehabilitation of Kikuyu

The task of rehabilitation of these people is one of the most pressing Christian responsibilities in Africa. A special working fund of $90,000 is being requested through Church World Service and the World Council of Churches. Scores of special workers are needed to work directly in the camps if they are qualified, or to replace experienced workers now engaged in other tasks, so that they in turn may be free for this crucial work.

The spiritual hunger and emptiness of the Kikuyu who turned in revulsion away from Mau Mau is indescribable. And the few workers now among them are staggered by the opportunity that is open just now, and that may not last long or come again. It is difficult to see what the future of the country of Kenya can be unless these fifty thousand people can be rapidly restored to normal society.

These are but glimpses of present situations against which we may try in some measure to forecast the things to come. Many other things should be mentioned—particularly the great advance in autonomy and self-government in West Africa, in those territories of British West Africa, a development that is being watched with both hope and concern in other parts of Africa.

The Way of Repentance

There are, I believe, many great sins of which we are guilty and which have brought great harm to Africa. To undo that harm goes far beyond the unaided power of the churches and mission bodies here represented. These sins are a reproach and a challenge to the whole church universal and to the conscience of Christian men and women wherever they may be. Only as we unite wholeheartedly to combat these evils can they be overcome.

The Sin of Racialism

The first of these is racialism. We must abolish racial discrimination and segregation wherever it is found and embrace the brotherhood that Christ sealed in his own blood. The apostle Paul in the first century of the Christian church was confronted with the racialism of the Jewish people on the one hand, and the cultural exclusiveness of the Greeks on the other.

He said that all of these things count for nothing before the throne of Christ, for he came to break down the middle wall of partition, and to make both one—neither Jew nor Greek, but a new creature in Christ. And so it must be with us.

The progress that has been made recently in this country has its repercussions in Africa, but so do our setbacks. The troubles over school desegregation in Baltimore and Washington were reported under large headlines in Johannesburg and Pretoria while I was there. Americans in Africa, presumably Christian in their private life, are far too quick to accept the segregationist attitudes of those about them. Our testimony in this matter must be unimpeachable. There is a real danger that Africans will lose patience with the white man's pretensions of friendship and concern, which are so often denied in practice, and turn in revulsion against the whole culture of the West. If that happens there will be a rejection of Christianity also, because Christianity, to the mass of Africans, is related still to the culture of the West and not thought of as Africa's faith.

The Sin of Destroyed Community

Second, we must abolish human exploitations and establish a community. I have already referred to the migrant labor in Africa, especially the system that sends boys and young men to work far from their own homes for long periods of time, and thus destroys home and family life for millions of people. This is probably the most flagrant social evil in Africa today—not excepting segregation. There is literally no hope of a positive social development nor a strong church in any country where such a system prevails.

We must turn our attention speedily to eradication of this evil and the substitution of family life in ordered communities if there is to be social health in Africa. To do this will require the cooperation of many other agencies besides the church. The most discouraging situation that one finds in Africa is the way in which each separate community thinks of itself apart from all the rest. Even missionaries sometimes, when I ask them the population of a town, give me the European population and forget that the total population of the community is at least ten times the figure they give me. The whole of Africa is divided according to these lines of race and culture. There is little prospect of genuine progress until these barriers are transcended.

There is need for more scientific study of these questions. Able scholars should be found and supported and encouraged in the work of the social sciences in Africa. There are some excellent institutes and institutions at work, any one of which could easily do a great deal more and better work than it has either staff or funds to undertake at present.

Visitation and exchange of personnel between different areas should be encouraged so that constructive developments can be made more widely known. That applies to missionaries, to government people, to employers, and many others who need to know what somebody else is doing successfully around the corner.

The Role of the Church

On the positive side, the church has an essential role to play in creating new bonds of unity and fellowship, a new sense of belonging, a new neighborliness grounded in the love of Christ, to replace the old sanctions of clan and tribe that no longer serve.

The National Council of Churches has given us a charter of action in this field. I want to read from the Statement of Christian Principles and Assumptions for Economic Life, adopted by the General Board on September 15 of this year:

"Applications of ethical principles in the economic order, paragraphs 4 and 5:

"Economic institutions should be judged also by their impact upon the family, which involves standards of living, hours of labor, stability of employment, provision for housing, and the planning of cities—especially in relation to their industrial development—and elimination of blighted areas."

It is a clear Christian responsibility to work against these special forms of economic injustice that are expressed through racial and other group discrimination. I should like somebody to take that whole document and translate it into its African equivalent, and then make use of it.

Speak with One Voice—Act with One Mind

In this hour when Africa needs, above all else, a powerful affirmation of the judgment and grace of God, we cannot speak with one voice nor act with one mind because we are divided. Only as we unite our voices through the Christian councils and similar agencies can we deal with governments from positions of strength on matters of public policy, of education, of health and welfare, and all the other matters in which the churches have a vital stake.

In the Crowded Ways

As we face our task in Africa, where should we place the emphasis? I believe that a high priority must be given to the towns and cities, the plantations and industrial centers, which are growing at an unbelievable rate all over Africa. Too often we have deliberately turned our backs on the city. Of course rural work is easier. Of course the cities are full of iniquity. But our people are going there in throngs and droves, and the church must go with them. Like a city church in this country, the African church must serve the needs of its parish, and those needs come to a focus at two points: worship and fellowship. Worship we have provided. Fellowship has been relatively neglected.

The African who comes into a big city for the first time must be one of the loneliest persons on earth. His home community was a network of social relations and mutual obligations. None of those ties goes with him to the city. He may find scarcely anyone with whom he can talk. He is in an alien world.

What these Africans need most is fellowship, neighborliness, a sense of belonging, a chance to put down roots and build themselves into a new community where they can feel at home once more. So within the urban church there must be groups and fellowship—young people's clubs and societies—and adult education activities, and classes serving different age and interest groups to help the individuals adjust themselves and to help one another in any number of different ways.

Where the church is reaching out in this way it is growing in power and influence. Where it neglects this side of its work it tends to become less and less significant in the total life of the community. Here and there governments and other agencies are attempting to provide community houses and welfare centers. The secularization of those activities deprives them of much of their effectiveness and value, and it deprives the church of one of its great functions in urban society.

Church—First Responsibility

A still higher priority must be given to the church itself
—this in two senses: First, the church must take prece-
dence in our thinking and our choosing over everything that
competes with it for attention and support. I do not question the value or even the necessity of all the various tasks
that engage us, but some of them could, if necessary, be
done by other agencies. But our first responsibility is to
implant in Africa a living church composed of men and
women who have found life and have been made new in our
Lord Jesus Christ, so that even apart from us the church
may continue to be the channel of his love and grace. Apart
from the church I see no hope for Africa.

Mission Loses Identity

The second way in which we must give prominence to the
church is in relation to the missions. Far too often we still
think of the mission first and the church second. I am convinced that the sooner the mission loses its identity com-
pletely and merges itself into the life of the African church,
the better God will be able to work through us. Too often
the mission remains the means by which foreign domination
of the church persists long after it should have been elim-
inated. We may be unconscious of it when, to our African
brethren, it has become a stumbling block and an offense.

One Church

I do not want to labor questions of mere organization, but
I believe they often point to something deeper. Twenty
years ago—in 1934—it was agreed in the Congo that the
missions should unite in building up one church, the Church
of Christ in Congo. Yet it is only this year that the first

tentative steps were taken to establish a central consultative council for that church, and to give it direct representation in the Congo Protestant Council. Must we move so slowly?

Or consider the Bacongo area within that church. Here is one continuous area occupied by one tribe, speaking the same language, but served by four Protestant missions—one Swedish, one British, and two American. Three of these four missions train their pastors and teachers in a single institution. All four are united in a central medical school in Africa. Yet the church of that area has no central conference, no internal organizational unity. Would it not serve the interests of the kingdom of God to develop a regional conference or synod for the whole area so that that church might speak and act on its own behalf rather than through four separate mission bodies? In matters such as these we must not delay overlong, for time is running out.

Leaders for Africa

Finally, we must give the highest priority to the provision of creative leadership. Far too many missionaries are engaged in humdrum tasks of secondary importance from which they should be freed for creative pioneering. Far too many Africans are working in secondary posts that do not challenge their powers of leadership or initiative, and they should be taking over major tasks that hitherto have been in missionary hands. We are far too hesitant to break with the inherited traditions of the task. Yet here also there are hopeful signs.

In Uganda I was the guest of an African minister, an able and devoted man who has recently succeeded a missionary as the head of a theological college. In Angola, where the number of missionaries we can send into the country is limited, more and more individuals are being freed from local station duties to give specialized oversight to one or another aspect of work for the whole area. Along with that there goes the development of rural centers, staffed by Africans and providing church, school, dispensary, and agricultural leadership to a circle of the villages embracing a considerable area.

In respect to leadership for the African church, we now have the benefit of the survey on the training of ministry, the ministry in Africa, conducted over a term of years under the direction of the International Missionary Council. The three reports of this study should be required reading for every board secretary and every missionary to Africa. One of the commissions limits itself to a single recommendation, which I quote:

"That not less than one-fourth of missionary personnel and efforts should be wholeheartedly directed to the training of ministers and of lay workers of the churches with whatever severe readjustments that change would require."

But missionaries must also be inspired and prepared for creativeness. We must help them see their task whole through studies such as this one on the training of the ministry; through opportunities for consultation and fellowship; through visits to significant pieces of work done by others; and through appropriate furlough study. It has even been suggested, and I think this is an important suggestion, that there might be established in Africa one or more ecumenical institutes or study communities, where a permanent residential staff, together with invited participants, would lead a changing group, including missionaries, nationals, and lay men and women, in a continuing study of the relevance of the Christian gospel to Africa's life and needs.

Above all else, there must be constant spiritual renewal

in order that the mind and spirit of Christ may triumph even in the weakness and human insufficiency of his servants. Our task is not to impose our pattern on Africa, but to disclose the pattern that God has prepared and ordained in Christ Jesus.

NOTE: The unabridged speech may be had by writing to the Division of Foreign Missions, National Council of Churches, 156 Fifth Avenue, New York 10, N. Y.

THOUGHT PROVOKERS

1. Is industrialization of Africa necessarily progress? Is it necessarily evil?

2. What are the first considerations that drive Africans to mines or industries?

3. How can the world church play a role in bridging the gap between the "sincere" white man who believes in segregation and the suspicious African?

4. Do you think that Africa can become a successful multi-racial society?

5. What does the author mean by "establishing a community"?

6. Is there any way that an American living in his own country may act so that he may have an influence on doing away with the slums of Johannesburg?

7. If major tasks of the mission are taken over by Africans, what role does the missionary play?

8. In a country needing services as desperately as Africa why does the author put the establishing of the church as the first task of the mission?

9. How does the concept of the world church change the concept of the task of the church in Africa?

**the pattern
of things to come
in latin america**

Dr. Stockwell's paper was given toward the end of the conference. There was not enough time to discuss it. A young man sat listening intently during the reading of the paper. After the paper was read another person murmured, "It seems that was more political pattern than religious." The young man was outraged.

"Did you hear that?" he asked a friend. "Did you hear that? He should live in Latin America a while and find where one leaves off and the other begins."

Latin America is a great territory. What is true in some of its countries is not true in others. But in all Latin American countries an intense political sense lies close to the surface. The church has to grow in the midst of this political atmosphere.

For that reason, if for no other, the student of missions will want to pay very close attention to the pattern of things to come in Latin America.

by B. Foster Stockwell

One of the outstanding North American specialists in Latin American studies has said recently that present-day political stability in Latin America is no greater than it was a hundred years ago, and that he sees only the dreary round of dictatorships and revolutions. One may cite chapter and verse to support such a thesis, but it seems to me unduly pessimistic.

Only a few weeks ago, Columbia University, as a part of its bicentennial celebration, called a conference on "Responsible Freedom in the Americas." Among the distinguished men who attended the conference and presented papers were five former presidents of Latin American countries and an Argentine Nobel prize winner in medicine. These men, some of whom have suffered exile for their liberal, democratic convictions, were realistic in their evaluation of the current situation, but were not pessimistic as to the future. One of the most eloquent addresses of the conference was delivered by Dr. Eduardo Santos, former President of Colombia. At the present time, Dr. Santos said, the Latin American countries are victims of the shocks of totalitarianisms from the right and from the left—and more from the right than from the left. "The banner of anti-communism in Latin America," he said, "is becoming a banner of pirates. We have fought communism passionately; for the first thing that communism does is to eliminate freedom. The Spanish Republic was never communistic, but the rule of Franco may become communist. In Italy communism is strong where fascism was strong. If dictators continue in Latin America, everything will be ready for communism. If we have no liberty, what is there to defend? Let us be anti-communist, but anti-communist liberals."

There were two important points on which these Latin American liberals seemed to be of one accord. First, they regard our North American fear of communism in Latin America as somewhat exaggerated. No one denies that there are communists in Latin America, but there are serious differences of opinion on the best way of meeting communism there. One way is to follow the Guatemala pattern and deploy all our diplomatic and military forces in the area to overturn a government that leans too decidedly toward communism. This immediately raises in the minds of our Latin American friends the specter of "the big stick" and is interpreted by them as a violation of our pledged word not to intervene in their internal affairs.

The other point on which Latin American liberals seem to be of one mind is that, if our country is to move effectively against the totalitarianism of the left in Latin America, it must be more in the economic and social field and less in the diplomatic and military. The sale or cession of arms to Latin American countries is decidedly not the best way to strengthen genuinely democratic forces there. Eduardo Santos, in the stirring address to which I have already referred, declared that there was no real reason for Latin Americans to arm. "Arms are the morphine of our continent. The purchase of arms is the greatest crime in Latin America. To arm our intolerance is the height of absurdity." The arms of Latin America can play no real part in an international conflict in the atomic age. But, unfortunately, these same arms become the means of quashing any movement toward more democratic government and of subjecting friendly peoples to fascist dictators.

Greater than the danger of communism in Latin America is the danger of poverty and ignorance and injustice, of fascism and clericalism and religious persecution. These things constitute the kind of soil in which the seeds of communism grow. Unless these dangers can be lessened, unless the roots of discontent and suffering can be destroyed, we can only expect their fruit in revolutions and communism. This is why many of our friends in Latin America have hailed the work of the Point Four Program. This is why others have appealed for a kind of Marshall Plan for the Americas. This was the plea made by Claude G. Bowers, former United States Ambassador to Chile, in the conference on "Responsible Freedom in the Americas."

"Communism in this hemisphere," he said, "cannot be decisively defeated by bayonets; guns may score a temporary triumph but in the end communism can only be defeated with bread. . . . The preservation of the freedoms is dependent on the lifting of the economic and social status of the masses. . . . A small part of the billions we have poured into Europe and Asia in preparation for a war that may never, never come, if used for the economic development of our immediate neighbors to the south, would have been worth five hundred divisions trying to hold back communism with the bayonet. . . . The reduction to a ridiculous figure of assistance to twenty-odd nations that are our immediate neighbors cannot, in my opinion, be justified by any rule of reason. . . . A Marshall Plan for South and Central America would be a mighty contribution to the preservation of the freedoms of the Western hemisphere."

Such a plan for economic cooperation ought to be undertaken, as Dr. Santos said, not on the basis of "charity" or "help," but as an expression of the same kind of statesmanship our country has displayed in Europe.

What has all this to do with our Protestant work in Latin America? Much in every way, for it provides the background of our work and defines our problems in the social and economic spheres. In the deepest sense, politics and religion are not far apart. Those of us who have lived for years in Latin America, and have observed at first hand the life of those countries, cannot but believe that there is a relation between the kind of religion they profess and the kind of social and political life they have. Roman Catholicism, when left to develop along its own lines, becomes a totalitarian form of religion. In Latin America this kind of religion has been on the side of totalitarian forms of government.

When these countries achieved their independence a century and a half ago, they had some of the finest leaders in this hemisphere—men who could stand beside the leaders of the North American revolution. But the great mass of people there had not been trained in those habits of life nor did they possess those qualities of character that undergirded political democracy; I mean personal conviction, unquestionable integrity, self-criticism, tolerance of divergent opinions, faith in the common man and his possibilities, readiness to sacrifice oneself for the common good, the spirit of team play. They adopted constitutions not unlike our own, but they lacked the substance of democracy in the education and history of their peoples. Democratic government flourishes where there is religious democracy. Revolution breaks out where the attempt is made to impose some kind of tyranny.

Protestantism in Latin America, with its democratic life and spirit, is doing its share in laying surer foundations for political democracy and international understanding. Those southern countries are passing through social and political struggles such as our forefathers passed through centuries ago. In that struggle Protestantism is on the side of real democracy; for in building sturdy Christian character, we are laying the spiritual foundations of a more stable political life.

THOUGHT PROVOKERS

1. If you accept the premise that political stability in Latin America is no greater than it was one hundred years ago, what reasons do you feel explain the situation?

2. Do you think that speeding up of technical assistance would be of great help against communism? Would it have any effect on religious growth?

3. Do you agree that the extreme "right" is a breeding place for communism?

4. What is meant in the statement, "Arms are the morphine of our continent"?

5. Do you agree that politics are molded by the religion of a country as well as religion by the politics?

6. How do you explain the fact that, while Latin America had some of the finest leaders in the world a century ago, there is little sign of democratic leadership today?

7. How can the mission program fit itself for service in the struggle toward democracy?

8. Do you feel that the Protestant faith has a unique contribution to make in Latin America today in its historical future? If so, why?

   *Throughout the conference there was talk of the way
churches and missions are working together. The ways of work
varied from sharing plans to conducting interdenominational
schools and conferences. Miss Glora Wysner of the
International Missionary Council told of the plan to intensify
the study of non-Christian religions. This will mean,
in some cases, the strengthening of schools already established;
in other cases, the setting up of studies. The series of
theological books prepared by the International Missionary
Council was reported—one off the press now, others to come.
This was a reminder that new Christians have had, in many
cases, few books to help them in their own theological
development and in preparing them to teach others. Regional
conferences were considered as a part of the pattern already
emerging. But the most significant reports were of those
practical cooperative efforts that fall into the pattern
of a scientific age. Mr. Burton Martin reported on one of
the most important.*

by W. Burton Martin

Today there will be made the first broadcast over radio station HLKY in Seoul, Korea, an event that is an outstanding example of the churches working together. Station HLKY is the first privately operated station to be granted a permit by the government of the Republic of Korea. In this joint project are united under the Korean Christian Council the four largest churches in Korea: the Presbyterian, Methodist, Holiness, and Salvation Army. The Methodist Church, the Presbyterian Church U. S., the Presbyterian Church U. S. A., the Australian Presbyterian Church, the United Church of Canada, and an Oriental missionary society have cooperated to bring this to pass.

I use this as an example because, first of all, it indicates that in the pattern of things to come there will be, and is, an increased awareness of the place of radio and film in communicating the Christian message. The nature of our world demands it. There may have been a time when we could wait and expect no change to take place in a village or country until the church went in and brought about another change. But that time is past. In ten countries in Africa that I visited last year, nine of those countries had governments actively at work in promoting broadcasting and in placing radio receivers out in the villages and hamlets. Of the ten countries visited, eight of them were actively at work with government mobile units, taking the message of the government, by film and filmstrip, into remote areas of the country. It is impossible to think of the church in our day failing to use these media of communication.

There are nine million radios in Japan. On the basis of averages, 45,000 of these would be in the homes of Christians, 8,955,000 in the homes and shops of non-Christians. In most countries of Latin America there are more radio receivers than the total combined daily circulation of newspapers. The second largest motion picture industry is not to be found in England, France, or Italy, but in India. It is as impossible to think of the church in our century failing to use these media as it is to think of Martin Luther failing to use the printing press.

In the second place, the station in Korea is part of the pattern of cooperative effort. I am not at all certain that the reason we are able to cooperate in the field of radio is primarily because of the fact that radio is a non-theological medium. I think that the bases of cooperation go deeper than that. When a man stands in his pulpit he surrounds it with evidence that makes him different from the man in the church across the street. Such evidence may be a baptismal pool or a baptismal font, a central pulpit or a central altar—any number of things that interpret our traditions.

When a man stands before a microphone he is not thinking of those things that make him different from others; he is thinking of the people he is seeking to reach. Radio is basically an evangelistic medium and one in which we can unite because of our common purpose in reaching men and women for Jesus Christ. The church is at its best when it confronts the non-Christian world in mission and in unity. And it is this confrontation of the non-Christian world by means of radio that draws us together and makes possible projects such as the one in Korea.

Did you ever hear a preacher at the close of his morning sermon turn to the congregation and say, "I hope you will be in church next Sunday morning. Go to the church of your choice"? Once he gets people into the sanctuary, he is pretty certain that he will try to get them back to that sanctuary on the next Lord's day. But you have heard again and again a radio program close with the words, "See a church next Sunday from the inside," or "Go to the church of your choice," for we are united in a sense of mission as we use this medium.

Radio broadcasting is a project of cooperative effort by Christians, whether they be missionaries, fraternal workers, or Nationals. We are committed to the proposition that in every country people should be permitted to have the opportunity of hearing the Christian message over the radio, in the language of the area, spoken by one for whom it is the native language, thus creating a sense of unity between listener and broadcaster.

Back in the fifteenth century Martin Luther was bold enough to use the printing press as an instrument in the hands of God. Today, by working together, we must capture the waves of the air for the glory of the Christian message.

THOUGHT PROVOKERS

1. How can one offset the proprietary denominational interest at home when a cooperative work—or a united church—comes into being where the denominations have been working?

2. Are there situations in which working alone—one denomination in an area—can still be so done that the church involved has a feeling of "togetherness"?

3. Do you see the use of the radio in bringing about such a "togetherness" even if the mission church is not part of the Christian cooperative supporting the radio?

4. Do you think that the variety of richness in churches will be strengthened or weakened by an emphasis on cooperation? If you feel that the richness will be less, do you think that the over-all gain will be greater than the loss?

Before a revolutionary change in a country there is often a recklessness about the populace. This is true in Western cities. It is even more true—or more apparent, perhaps, is a better word—in Eastern cities. Before Shanghai fell even the pedicab men seemed to be operating on principles of direction unknown to any but themselves. Businessmen, in the midst of a trade, would pause, look ahead, and let their minds fall into silence. During all this a group of young Christian women were carrying on, as usual, their program for factory girls and women.

At that time—it may still be true—many of the girls in the Shanghai factories were working a ten-hour day, a ten-day stretch. Most of them were young. They were a force that the communists could reach easily and effectively with propaganda. They were illiterate. The young Christian women went to the factory gates and invited the girls to come to their rooms to learn reading and writing.

They came—many of them.

The rooms were up steep stairs. Beds were pushed aside, and stools and boxes brought in for seats. Blackboards were set up. And in the evenings—after ten hours of work—young girls were initiated into the mystery of marks on a page that stood for ideas.

The young Christian women had made up rather primitive readers. The characters used were the thousand characters that had been developed by James Yen. In the pattern of American readers, the stories used the characters (words) that had just been learned by the young students. Many a

Christian teaching was incorporated in the little, rude books. One page told of the hand: "This is the character for the hand; this is the character for the fingers," and a little story of what divine work a hand can do in the service of the world.

The young Christians were not naïve. They knew that at any moment the city could fall. That it would fall eventually they had no doubt. But—with irresolution around them—they were settling to their task of teaching illiterate girls reading and writing—a long, tedious process. "It is said," remarked one of these young women, "that at particular times in a person's life he is more capable of taking in new ideas than others. One of those times is when a person learns the meaning of what is written on a page. We are putting Christian ideas before these girls knowing that, whether they live by them or not, there is little chance they will forget them."

A revolution moved about that room in the old city of Shanghai. But a revolution was within the room, too.

* * * * *

In a South American country, where the leading religion was showing more and more repressive tendencies toward the minority religions, the missionaries were almost in despair. In the early days a Protestant church had been built but it seemed to be at a standstill. The atmosphere was hostile toward reaching even those men and women who had no religious ties at all.

In the midst of this a book was translated into Spanish and published. It was published over considerable protest by some of the missionary forces. It was a compilation of the speeches of men at a great meeting held in the United

States. It was called *Christian Bases of World Order*. Some of the missionaries said that the book would be over the heads of the Protestant group and that those who could understand it would never see the book. But it was published and in due course of time turned up on the bookstalls of the country of which we speak. By some chance it fell into the hands of one of the leading women of the capital—a conservative Roman Catholic who had a good deal of influence with the hierarchy. In speaking later to a school mistress who was a Protestant, the Catholic woman said, "It was as if I had opened a door and saw a vision beyond all my dreams of what religion could mean to the world. I feel I must gather the women I know together and tell them of this vision. I have already told my own priest and he agrees with me that our church must in this land take heed of these things or the religious soul will die."

This woman could never be reached by the missionary in person. It is probable that she could never be turned toward an Evangelical religion. But through a book she was brought in contact with a new view of religion in its relation to man. She gave herself to the purpose of liberalizing the atmosphere about her. How effective she was one cannot tell. The atmosphere became more liberal, but that change may have been on its way. But even if she had no discernible effect, she herself had been revolutionized in her religious thought—a door had been opened that, though she may never go through the door, can never be closed to her.

*   *   *   *   *

During the years since the Second World War the Islamic religion has seen a great resurgence. Even in Turkey, where religion has been separated from the state for over a quarter of a century, there are manifestations of the growing interest in religion.

In the midst of this growth of interest a young man came to one of the missionaries and asked for a religious book to read.

The missionary went to his bookshelf and, without any hesitation, gave the young man a small book. The book had been printed by a Christian book company. It was well printed on thick white paper with ink that stood up sharply from the pages. The young man looked at the title, which announced that the book was the birth song of the prophet, written in the tenth century by one of the major writers of the Islamic world.

The young man was surprised.

"Do you know the song?" the missionary asked him.

"No, I've never heard of it."

"You should know it," said the missionary. "It is said to be one of the most beautiful prayers ever written in any religion."

Then, to the first book, he added one of the Gospels.

"I feel," said the missionary almost defiantly, "that a great part of the Christian witness is to give back to the non-Christian some of the beauties produced by his own faith of which he may not know."

*   *   *   *   *

Immediately after the war the Christians of the Kikuyu tribe in the Kenya Colony, East Africa, experienced a religious revival. It came just at the time when the nationalist movement was on the increase in the colony. Suspicion of the Westerner was everywhere. Many of the tribesmen felt that the European had deprived them of their lands.

The non-Christian Africans began to draw into a compact group, antagonistic and hostile, not only to the ones who they felt had despoiled them, but also to all Westerners and to the Christians who had come under the influence of missionaries. The terrorist group of the Kikuyas, called Mau Mau, declared war on all Europeans, and vented their anger as well on the African Christians, who refused to join the terrorists.

Christians walking on lonely roads were set upon and killed in a most horrible way. But the church of the Christians seems to have conquered, in some way, the fear that one could expect them to have. The women have arranged to meet early in the morning—at five-thirty—for their devotions. When they have been threatened they have continued with their religious observances. Some women who have been told that they must renounce their faith or die have made arrangements for their funerals and calmly continued to assert their faith. One such woman, when asked how she could remain so calm, replied, "Whether we live or die we are the Lord's, so I am content and leave everything in his hands."

Waruhiu, a well known Christian chief, tried to effect better relationships between Africans and whites. On one occasion, he invited local farmers to attend a sports meeting at one of the schools in his province. At the end of the sports events he stepped forward and indicated a log that lay at his feet.

"Come," he called to ten white men. "See if you can lift this log."

The white men tugged and pulled, but the log remained on the ground.

"Now," he called to the Africans. "Let us see if you can do better than the white men."

You know the answer. The log remained where it was. Then he suggested all twenty work at the log and the log was moved.

The crowd was delighted and got the point.

Today Christian Africans are patrolling the roads, are moving into the barbed-wire enclosures where the convicted terrorists are held to carry the gospel, and are working with the missionaries to rehabilitate a frightened and hostile people. Their greatest job, they report, is to fight hate.

From the office of the World Council in Geneva comes the report that "in a good many places in Kenya, Christianity is stronger than it has ever been. As a whole, Christians seem to have found an inner victory over fear, which has given them confidence in spite of persecution."

* * * * *

"This is the Voice of Protestantism . . ." Another Sunday morning program was under way. Hundreds of listeners in Argentina and Uruguay were again tuned to CW23, Radio Cultural de Salto, for the weekly radio program of Christian music and meditation.

Mr. Eugene L. Stockwell tells the story of the radio through the last two years.

"We started in May [two years ago]. Throughout the entire month we did not receive a single letter. No one ever seemed interested to ask for the free pamphlets we offered. . . . But in June we received our first letter, a long and glowing message of gratitude, which warmed our hearts and inspired us to continue. Slowly but surely other letters began to come in. Some expressed thanks for the program. Others wanted pamphlets. Others asked for the New Testament. Some presented questions about Protestantism and religion in general. Several set forth gnawing personal problems, 'I am engaged to a Roman Catholic man, but I want to be a good Protestant. Shall I marry him?'

"We answered every letter personally, attempting both to fulfill all requests and to open up the way for future help if desired. In several cases our first answering letter to a mere request for a pamphlet led to subsequent letters presenting a personal problem.

"As we traveled occasionally to interior towns we always were greeted with references to our program. It was clear that many listened who never wrote letters to us. The word was passed along that our program was on the air, and friends of friends began to swell our radio audience. It seemed that God was using our program, in ways we could not have expected, to help people and to make known the Christian message."

*   *   *   *   *

In South India the Book Team sets out very early to avoid the heat of the day. Into the car go posters, literacy charts, books, even games for children. The Indian road is a friendly road. The people gather to talk as the car stops.

"Do you know how to read?" one of the team asks a young man.

"Yes," he says.

The member gives a pamphlet to the man. It is obvious the man does not know how to read. The pamphlet is held the wrong way. There is an embarrassed laugh as the crowd roars.

"You see," says the man, "it is a shame not to read now. Everyone in India, now that it is free, should be able to read. But how can all of us be taught?"

At the end of its journey, the team is assisted by village Christians. Books are set out for those who know how to read—for both Christians and non-Christians. Classes for the illiterate are set up under the trees. An old man stops at the edge of the class and is invited to try to read.

"I am too old."

"No one is too old who has his eyes and his mind."

The old man suggests that when the others eat he will come. Another man rises to read. He had had his first lesson on the last visit of the team.

Under other trees young Christians are learning to teach others. There is great earnestness and much discussion. Ideas have carried far because of some of the books left behind on the last trip. Men and women, used to discussing the events of a small village, discuss the ideas in a book.

As the evening comes the Book Team picks up its posters and charts and leaves for its headquarters. One member of the team points out the figure of a little boy—silhouetted against the sky on a hillock—lost in a book.

"Can you keep a village supplied with Christian literature?" asks a visitor. "Isn't it dangerous in a revolutionary time like this to teach people to read when you cannot control their reading?"

The leader of the team replies, "Reading is a gift we dare not withhold from men and women. We must, if we are Christian, teach and take the chance that the gift may be used wrongly."

*   *   *   *   *

In Uruguay the mission on wheels started for the northernmost part of the country. At night it reached its first stopping place, the city of Salto. The loud-speaker was hitched up to the microphone and the people in the streets of Salto heard, the first time for many of them, a Protestant message. They lingered—perhaps first attracted by the novelty but eventually caught, some of them, by the message itself.

The next day the mission stopped where the farmers worked in the fields and broadcast fine church music. The farmers came to the road and asked to be spoken to. The sermon was close to the problems of their daily lives. The farmers asked where they could get more teaching when the mission had gone its way. Before the wheels were rolling a nucleus of a Christian fellowship, which grew into a new church, had been formed.

Out of this one trip two new churches came into being.

*   *   *   *   *

Malaya, after the Second World War, was left with a "squatter" population of nearly 500,000. Some of them had fled to Malaya to escape war. Some had been driven out of other countries. Whatever the reason there they were, living in little shacks on whatever land they could find. They had no schools, they had no doctors. Some of them had no work. They were made for the communists of Malaya.

The government was aware of that. Resettlement communities appeared almost overnight. Where yesterday there was a rubber estate on a patch of jungle, today there is the beginning of a community of from five thousand to twenty thousand people.

The Christian church in Malaya has launched a program to start schools, clinics, and churches in these new towns. Of course the program is too big for the church of Malaya—

or indeed for any one denomination. Since most of the squatters are Chinese the missionaries from China are most useful. The China Inland Mission and the Church Missionary Society are but two of the many who are working to make these new communities Christian communities. In some of the communities the people built their own church out of their own funds.

There are many new experiences in a resettlement community. One is piped water; another is raising pigs under the direction of a farm cooperative. One is voting—sometimes for the first time in one's life—for the governors of the settlement. There is, sometimes, the first experience with Christianity. And there is also a first experience, for many Malayan Christians, with home missions on a vast scale. These people could not have been served by a single group. The task is overwhelming. Now today the church moves forward united in its task to make Christ known to the uprooted people in a Far Eastern land.

*   *   *   *   *

In the foot hills above Beirut there is a Y.W.C.A. camp for Lebanese girls. One weekend some World Y.W.C.A. visitors met with the girls at the camp and discussed some of the policies of the Y.W.C.A. One policy has always been the "inclusiveness" of the Y.W.C.A.'s program and its concern for all people. Some did not care for it.

"How," said one, "would you like to have a Jew come to one of our clubs?"

It was a time when feeling ran high.

One girl thrust forth her slender brown arm and said, "I have one answer. The blood of the Arabs runs through that arm."

"And I," said another girl, thrusting forth her arm as vigorously, "have another answer, for the blood of a Christian runs through *that* arm. Therefore, I could not close a club to a Jew."

THOUGHT PROVOKERS

1. In the face of the scarcity of missionary personnel, do you think that there is place for work in a "hopeless" situation, as far as winning converts to Christ is concerned?

2. How do you justify the publishing of books for men and women outside the faith through mission funds?

3. What do you think of a mission policy of bringing to the non-Christian the riches of his own religion?

4. Should the Christian—new in the faith and set in a country hostile to the Westerner—be expected to witness to the supraracial character of Christianity? If your conclusion is "yes," do you think that there are any limits to that witnessing?

5. How much stress do you think the mission program should give to radio? Do you feel that there is wisdom in keeping the programs in the hands of the Christians of the country? If so, why? Are there any contributions that the radio can make to reaching a larger group of people that cannot be made in any other way?

6. Do you agree that all men and women have the right to learn reading and writing no matter what are the dangers when they become literate?

7. Does the cooperative effort of a national home mission society and two foreign missionary societies seem a workable pattern? Has any part of this book suggested how it can be done? Does it suggest a future pattern to you?

8. Are there evidences that the Christian church can grow in the midst of revolution? What factors in some revolutions may stop the growth of the church?

In these pages there has been a great emphasis upon the responsibility carried, or to be carried, today by the younger churches. The missionaries have stressed the need for the development of native leaders for the responsibility. The churchmen from mission lands have stressed the eagerness with which they have welcomed the opportunity for responsibility. The man of the country speaks in a tongue that can never be equaled by a foreign tongue. He thinks in the figures of speech, in the inherited experience of the land.

I can remember once hearing an African preacher call out one word. It was, as I remember it, *"Tchah."* It was apparent from the nudges and the looks on the faces of the audience that they had caught the allusion. When the word was translated for me it carried no thought at all. It was, again I speak from hazy memory, the name of a flying insect that was considered a delicacy in Africa. But this word —one word—called forth a folk story so close to the African that nothing more was needed to be said to drive home the point. It was as if one of our own preachers said, "the quality of mercy . . .," something that would be quite incomprehensible, uncompleted as it is, to a foreigner who might understand the words but not the allusion.

In the great non-Christian world, so one after another of these papers say, such complete understanding of allusions is almost imperative. Such accord is necessary in all the works of a mission. A diagnosis of a sick man may be quite difficult for a highly trained doctor from another land, when the doctor of the country can catch a word, an expression on the face, a twist of the head that will suggest to him what the disease may be. Even in the higher institutions of learning in the mission land the teacher of the country may be able to throw light on some abstract bit of knowledge in a way that a great foreign scholar could not equal.

In the pattern of things to come this is taken into account, not just to give the man of the country his full share in the work of the extension of the Kingdom, but to make the extension of the Kingdom more possible.

This does not mean that the task is to be left only to the man of the country. It happens, occasionally, that the very difficulty of understanding the foreign missionary, the strain that comes from trying to grasp the meaning gives at times greater light than if the words were more homely. Often the missionary has special skills in which his own country excels. There is a compulsion here for him to share the skills if the Kingdom is to come, and a compulsion for the young Christian to seek to assimilate the skills. It seems to me, too, that the missionary who comes from a Christian church that has been long established has a gift to contribute through the very ease he feels in Christian life. It is true that the new convert sometimes catches a glow as the new truth breaks on him that the older Christian may never have. But the glow, the very heat of the glow, needs to be tempered by the ease, the almost matter-of-factness with which the old Christian accepts the revelation of the Spirit as a natural phenomenon.

Someone said not long ago, speaking of work in a mission field, that the communication of the gospel was like the co-ordination of a ball team. There had to be a pitcher, but there had to be a catcher, too. The insinuation was that in non-Christian lands the catcher was missing. Now the truth of the matter is that when something of substance comes toward you your hands come up almost instinctively to catch it. It may, of course, fall through your fingers. But given such an instinct one need not despair that the pitcher will always throw his ball in vain. There are always some hands skillful enough to close around the object.

The pattern of things to come seems to indicate that both young churchmen and older churchmen are needed to throw the ball, each with his own type of skill. Both throw the ball expecting it to be caught.

The advantage of the two working together is the recognition of each one's skill. And it is quite possible that out of the recognition will come a fused skill that is beyond the sum of the two skills.

The revelation of the world church, of the world mission, is in its very beginning. One can see this by reading the papers in this book. But with *all* members of the church working at the mission of the church the revelation will become clearer. Part of the light, so these papers seem to say, will come from the experience of working together at a common task. Part of it will come from the impact of the Christian world upon the non-Christian. And here we go back again to one of the papers at the very beginning of this volume. The light will become brighter partly from "the acts of justice and kindness" of the non-Christian world itself, recognized through the impact. This is a very new idea brought out at this particular conference, the recognition of the light that can be found in the non-Christian world. But—and the papers here never lose sight of the fact—the full revelation of the church itself will never become entirely known until this light becomes part of that church.

This book is a tale of compulsion, the compulsion to share

the knowledge of Jesus Christ. It is also a book that seeks to find how to share the knowledge in a way that will cause that knowledge to become part of the man who hears it. In some papers there are theological or philosophical terms, it is true. But underneath one can feel the will to state the truth as simply as it was stated to a handful of fishermen. You will remember that truth was understood by them. The pattern of things to come is founded on the belief in the power of all men and women, in no matter what part of the world, to see the light of truth.

Whence cometh the power? The answer that the Christian gives to that question makes the peoples of the world one in spiritual heritage.

WHO'S WHO

RAMCHUNDRA S. BHANDARE

The recipient of an ecumenical scholarship under the World Council of Churches, he is in the United States under the sponsorship of the National Christian Council of India, taking postgraduate work in theology at Union Seminary, Dayton, Ohio. He holds a B.D. degree from the United Theological College, Bangalore. He served as traveling secretary of the Student Christian Movement in Western and Central India. He will return to Western India where he will supervise a whole district, with its many village churches, a position formerly held by an American missionary.

DR. GEORGE W. CARPENTER

Executive secretary, Africa Committee, Division of Foreign Missions, NCCC; a graduate of Colgate Rochester Theological Seminary, he holds a B.S. in Civil Engineering and a Ph.D. in Education from Yale University. In 1925 he was appointed missionary to Africa by the American Baptist Foreign Mission Society. In 1926 he was designated to serve on the faculty of the Union Evangelical Training Institute of Kimpese, Belgian Congo. Before returning to the States he was Managing Director of La Librairie Evangelique au Congo, in Leopoldville.

DR. ALFORD CARLETON

For thirty years a member of the Near East Mission of the American Board serving in Turkey and Syria; president of Alleppo College in Syria for seventeen years; consultant to the Ford Foundation for its Near East program. At present he is executive vice-president, American Board of Commissioners for Foreign Missions, Congregational Christian Churches, Boston; and a member of the Executive Board, Division of Foreign Missions, NCCC.

DR. RAYMOND A. DUDLEY

Secretary for India and Ceylon, American Board of Commissioners for Foreign Missions, Congregational Christian Churches; he is the retiring chairman, Division of Foreign Missions, NCCC, a post he has held for two years. He was a missionary to India from 1919 to 1943 working primarily on village education and evangelism.

DR. PETER EMMONS

Minister of Westminster Presbyterian Church, Scranton, Pennsylvania; president of Board of Foreign Missions, Presbyterian Church, U. S. A.; member of the Board of Trustees of Princeton Theological Seminary since 1925 and president of that board since 1949.

C. I. ITTY

At present studying at Union Theological Seminary; a member of the Syrian Orthodox Church in India; as a staff member of the Indonesian Christian Movement he visited almost all parts of the country; sent to Indonesia as a missionary by the Church in India; under appointment by the Y. M. C. A. to return to Indonesia to serve its youth program.

JOHN KAEMMER

Methodist missionary to Southeast Africa; volunteered for short term service in 1951 and has served for three years in Mozambique, Africa. His special training has been in the field of music; is now a student in Boston School of Theology. Upon completion of his theological training, he plans to return to Africa for full time missionary work.

Dr. Carl D. Kriete

Missionary under the Board of the Evangelical Church; during the early years of his missionary career he served as an evangelistic missionary in the Aivu-Wakamatsu village of northern Japan. Because of his linguistic abilities, he became an outstanding preacher in Japan in the decade before the outbreak of the war. He served as president of Mijagi Women's College, located in the city of Sendai in northern Japan. He was a member of the Commission of Six (missionaries) representing North American Protestantism sent to Japan to resume relationship with the church in that country. Until he retired in 1954 he served as counselor to the Protestant schools in Japan, carrying also administrative responsibilities in connection with the missionary organizations associated with the Church of Christ in Japan.

Dr. Rajah Manikam

Joint secretary in East Asia of the World Council of Churches and the International Missionary Council. Elected president of the Federation of Lutheran Churches in India at its triennial conference early in January. Member of the Madhya Pradesh (Central Provinces) Evangelical Lutheran Church.

W. Burton Martin

Secretary of the Audio Visual Division of the Board of Foreign Missions of the Presbyterian Church, U. S. A., since 1952; executive secretary of the Radio, Audio Visual Education and Mass Communications Committee (RAVEMCCO) of the Division of Foreign Missions, NCCC/USA; co-chairman of the World Committee for Christian Broadcasting; formerly a missionary in China.

Dorothy McConnell

Editor of *World Outlook,* official mission paper of the Methodist Board of Missions, and secretary for literature of that board. Has visited all mission stations of the Methodist Board except those in Korea; served as a consultant to the United States delegation at the setting up of the United Nations in San Francisco, April, 1945.

Dr. David G. Moses

Principal of Hislop College, Nagpur, India, a vice-chairman of the International Missionary Council, at present a Henry W. Luce visiting professor of World Christianity, Union Theological Seminary, New York.

The Rt. Rev. Lesslie Newbigin

Born in England; M. A. Cambridge; served as Student Christian Movement Secretary in England, then became a missionary for the Church of Scotland; he later served as its Candidates' Foreign Secretary; now Bishop of the Church of South India.

Dr. B. Foster Stockwell

Secretary to John R. Mott from 1920-22; in 1925 won Jacob Sleeper Fellowship conferred by Boston University to study abroad. His field of labor from 1926-32 was the Union Theological Seminary, Buenos Aires, Argentina. Directed the translation of Comentario Biblical de Abingdon in 1937. Delegate to International Missionary Council meeting, Madras, India, 1938.

Dr. Rolf A. Syrdal

Mission secretary of the Evangelical Lutheran Church; chairman of the Division of Foreign Missions and vice-chairman of the Executive Board.

TYPE: ELEVEN POINT O. S. #7, LEADED TWO POINTS.

COMPOSITION, PRINTING, AND PAPER BINDING:

THE EVANGELICAL PRESS, HARRISBURG, PENNSYLVANIA.

BOARD BINDING: CHARLES H. BOHN AND COMPANY, NEW YORK.

JACKETS AND PAPER COVERS: AFFILIATED LITHOGRAPHERS, INC.

NEW YORK. PAPER: WARREN'S #66 ANTIQUE.

TYPOGRAPHIC DESIGN: DOROTHY PAPY

BINDING: LOUISE E. JEFFERSON